CAMBRIDGE INTRODUCTION TO WORLD HISTORY
GENERAL EDITOR · TREVOR CAIRNS

GANDHI

F. W. Rawding

CAMBRIDGE UNIVERSITY PRESS
Cambridge
London   New York   New Rochelle
Melbourne   Sydney

Drawings by Mark Peppé
Maps by Reg Piggott

Published by the Press Syndicate of the University of Cambridge
The Pitt Building, Trumpington Street, Cambridge CB2 1RP
32 East 57th Street, New York, NY 10022, USA
10 Stamford Road, Oakleigh, Melbourne 3166, Australia

© Cambridge University Press 1980

First published 1980
Third printing 1986

Printed in Great Britain by
Ebenezer Baylis & Son Limited
The Trinity Press, Worcester, and London

Library of Congress Cataloguing in Publication Data
Rawding, F. W.
Gandhi.
(Cambridge introduction to the history of mankind: Topic book)
1. Gandhi, Mohandas Karamchand, 1869–1948.
2. Statesman – India – Biography.
DS481.G3R3676   954.03′5′0924 [B]   79-11008
ISBN 0 521 20715 0

Illustrations in this volume are reproduced by kind permission of the following:
Front cover, pp. 19, 26 (centre), 31 (above), 34, 36, 38, 44 (right) BBC Hulton Picture Library; pp. 4, 33 Illustrated London News; pp. 5, 15 (left), 26 (left and right), 28 (above), 39 (right), 41, 45, 46, 47 Gandhi National Museum; p. 6 British Library; pp. 7 (left), 29, 32, 39 (left) India Office Library and Records; pp. 7 (right), 17, 28 (below) Camera Press; p. 12 Royal Geographical Society; pp. 13, 14 (right), 16 Mansell Collection; p. 14 (left) Archives Department, Westminster City Libraries; p. 15 (right) London Borough of Hammersmith and Fulham Public Libraries; p. 18 Cambridge University Centre for South Asian Studies; pp. 21, 25 Local History Museum, Durban; p. 22 photograph Cambell Collections, University of Natal; p. 24 Africana Museum, Johannesburg; p. 31 (below) Faculty of Archaeology and Anthropology, Cambridge; p. 37 (left) Punch, photograph Cambridge University Library; p. 37 (right) Press Association; pp. 43, 44 (left) Keystone Press Agency. Back cover Bildarchiv Preussischer Kulturbesitz; p. 3 Mani Bhavan Gandhi Sangrahalaya.

front cover: *Mohandas Gandhi, about 1930, when he was at the height of his political powers.*

back cover: *British lions baffled by Gandhi's strange methods of resistance. A cartoon from the German magazine 'Simplicissimus', 1931.*

A memorial plaque of Gandhi in the prayer hall at Mani Bhavan in Bombay.

Contents

The Mahatma *p.4*

1   Childhood and youth *p.5*

2   Mohandas in England *p.13*

3   Failure in India *p.17*

4   Conflict in South Africa *p.20*

5   Mohandas returns to India *p.27*

6   The parting of the ways *p.32*

7   The salt tax Satyagraha *p.36*

8   The Round Table Conference, 1931 *p.38*

9   The campaign for the Harijans *p.40*

10   War and independence *p.41*

11   Hatred and partition *p.45*

12   The legacy of the Mahatma *p.48*

The Mahatma
Gandhi's funeral pyre on the banks of the Jumna River near Delhi. Thousands of people dressed in white watched while the body of Gandhi, known as the Mahatma, or Great Soul, was burned in the flames.

On 30 January 1948 Jawaharlal Nehru, Prime Minister of India, broadcast to the nation, telling the people of the death of Mohandas Gandhi at the hand of an assassin. He said 'The light has gone out of our lives and there is darkness everywhere and I do not know what to tell you or how to say it. Our beloved leader Bapu, as we call him, the father of our nation is no more.'

As Indian men and women wept and wailed, representatives of all the peoples and of all the religions of mankind mourned also. One of the most influential men in the world had passed away.

He was not rich – he dressed in the simple home-made cotton clothes of the peasant. He was not impressive to look at – he was small and ugly and even ridiculous in the presence of the great among whom he moved. He had no armed followers but he had mobilised a whole people, one fifth of the human race, and with the weapons of truth and non-violence he removed from India the forces of occupation of a foreign empire. He had brought the conscience of the British people to the point at which, having fought a World War in the name of freedom for themselves and for others, they could no longer deny freedom to the people of India. Throughout the struggle Gandhi's most powerful weapon was his willingness to die for his beliefs, and this he had now done. The body on the pyre was not, therefore, an old and worn-out shell but an offering of himself for the poor, the oppressed and the humble of all the world.

1 Childhood and youth

Gujarat

Mohandas Karamchand Gandhi was born on 2 October 1869 in the little town of Porbandar on the Kathiawar Peninsula of Western India. The name Mohandas, Slave of Mohan, or of Krishna (the Hindu god's other name), was to be a summary of his life. Krishna, in the holy Hindu book *Bhagavad Gita*, teaches his followers: 'Non-violence, truth, freedom from anger, renunciation, serenity, sympathy for all beings, gentleness, forgiveness, fortitude, freedom from pride – these are the treasures of the man who is born for heaven.'

Mohandas's father, Karamchand Gandhi, was the Dewan or Prime Minister of the little princely state of Porbandar, which was hardly bigger than the town itself, standing on the edge of the Arabian Sea. As Dewan he was responsible for the management of all the affairs of the state including taxation, law and order and so on. Karamchand was an experienced civil servant and from time to time worked also in some other nearby states.

In the Hindu caste system there are four principal castes. The Brahmins, most senior, are religious teachers and scholars. The Kshatriyas, next in rank, are traditionally warriors and from among them come the kings and princes. The Vaisyas are next; they are merchants, small landholders and clerks. Finally, least in rank, are the Sudras who are craftsmen and peasants performing certain services for the others. The name Gandhi means 'grocer', so the family of Mohandas was Vaisya, and not very distinguished in the caste sense, even though they were quite wealthy and had some lands and property.

In his book *An Autobiography: the Story of my Experiments with Truth*, Mohandas writes of his father: 'he never had any ambition to gather riches and left us very little'. The family was orthodox Hindu of the sect of the god Vishnu called Vaishnava. The Hindu religion apparently has many gods and

right: *Karamchand Gandhi.* The inscription was written by Mohandas and reads 'Mohandas falls at his feet'.

below: *Krishna and Arjuna (a hero of Hindu mythology) in their chariot. This miniature is from an early eighteenth-century manuscript of the Bhagavad Gita from Kashmir.*

goddesses, but these can be understood as representing the different powers and qualities of one complete divine power. The aspect of God most revered by the Gandhis is the God of Mercy who preserves mankind. From time to time, looking with pity upon the woeful state of the affairs of men, Vishnu comes into the world to lead us back to goodness. In one of these incarnations he is Krishna, in another Rama and so on. The kind of Hinduism in which Mohandas was brought up, therefore, was based upon the concept of a loving relationship between God and mankind, and in that respect it was rather like Christianity.

His mother, Putlibai, was a deeply religious woman who constantly recited the prayer, 'Krishna the Lord is my only refuge'. Of her Mohandas writes: 'the outstanding impression my mother made upon me was that of saintliness. She would take the most difficult vows and keep them without flinching.'

Another important religious influence on the life of Mohandas was that of the Jainas. They belong to a very small but ancient sect, similar to Buddhism and dating from about 300 BC. The chief doctrine of the Jainas is non-violence to any living creature. The sect has strong roots in Gujarat, the part of India where Mohandas was born, and it has influenced the character of Hinduism there.

Mohandas was a shy, solitary little boy and not very good at school. He writes of himself as he was when he was twelve: 'My books and my lessons were my sole companions. I was frightened in case anyone should poke fun at me.' He also tells of his childish faults, like smoking against the wishes of his parents, and of the shame he experienced in deceiving them. It was this shame and his love for them, rather than fear of punishment, which caused him to give up the habit. He appears at this time to have been a very sensitive boy, trying hard to be truthful but too upset if his teachers corrected him. He did not enjoy games but used to go for long walks in the countryside and became very fit and wiry. But

A guru, or teacher, with his pupils, a drawing made in Benares, about 1818.

Hindu weddings are still celebrated with traditional customs. Here the Prince of Bikaner and his bride are bound by a cord in a ritual union known as the kankana dharana.

he was quite untypical of boys of his age and was already forming a very independent and unusual character.

At the age of thirteen, according to the custom of those days, he was married to Kasturbai, the daughter of a merchant of Porbandar. Of his marriage he writes:

'Marriage among Hindus is no simple matter. The parents of the bride and groom often bring themselves to ruin over it. Months are taken up over the preparations, making clothes and ornaments and in preparing meals. My marriage meant no more to me than the prospect of good clothes to wear, drum beating, marriage processions and rich dinners. I can picture to myself even today how we sat on our wedding dais, how we performed the Seven Steps, how we put the sweet wheat cake into each other's mouths and how we began to live together.'

It was the expense involved in this sort of marriage which reduced the fortune of the Gandhi family.

Mohandas and Kasturbai were very fond of each other though they were both strong-willed and determined to have their own ways. They frequently quarrelled. The marriage, which became a great love in spite of continual storms, lasted sixty-two years until Kasturbai's death.

Looking back on his childhood marriage Mohandas condemned Hindu society for the cruelty of the custom. It disrupted his studies, ended his childhood and brought him abruptly to the responsibilities of an adult before he was ready to perform them properly.

One of his friends at the High School in Rajkot, where his father had moved on promotion to another official appointment, was Sheikh Mehtab, a Muslim boy. He was tall and strong and a fine athlete and Mohandas envied him. He writes that at that time he was afraid of ghosts and snakes and even of the dark. 'My friend knew all these weaknesses of mine. He told me that he could hold a live snake in his hand and that he did not believe in ghosts. All this was, of course, the result of eating meat.' Mohandas had never tasted meat, for his family, like all orthodox Hindus, was very strictly vegetarian. Sheikh Mehtab argued that most Indians are small and weak because they do not eat meat. At school the boys used to sing a jingle:

'Behold the Mighty Englishman,
He rules the Indian small.
Because he is a meat eater
He is five cubits tall.'

opposite: Villages in Gujarat and in many other parts of India look like this. Eighty per cent of the people live a simple life, which has not changed much for hundreds of years. In spite of some advance in mechanisation and the use of fertilisers, farming, for the vast majority, is still carried out with traditional tools and methods.

Finally Mohandas was talked into tasting meat to see if it would make him strong. He ate some goat meat, found it tough and unpleasant and felt guilty about deceiving his parents. He continued to eat meat secretly from time to time for about a year but always felt that he was hurting his mother and father. Then he made up his mind never to eat meat again.

At about this time Mohandas stole a gold coin from his elder brother, but felt so much remorse that he made up his mind never to steal again. He also decided to confess the deed to his father. Not able to bring himself to speak of it because of the pain his confession would cause, he wrote a letter to his father, who was ill in bed at the time, and watched full of shame while it was read.

> 'He read it through and pearl drops of tears trickled down his cheeks wetting the paper. For a moment he closed his eyes in thought and then tore up the note.
> I also cried, seeing my father's agony. Those pearl drops of love cleansed my heart and washed my sin away. This was for me an object lesson in Ahimsa.'

Ahimsa means love and non-violence. Mohandas learned from his father's act of love and forgiveness that the power of Ahimsa has no limits and that it purifies everything it touches. Throughout all his future life Mohandas kept the promises made in boyhood.

In 1885 his father died. Mohandas was with Kasturbai at the time and he always reproached himself for not being with his father to lighten the burden of death. In 1887 he passed his high school examinations and was sent to College in Bombay. His English was not very good (the language of his family was Gujarati) and he found life at College strange and difficult. He was disheartened and returned home after only a term. A family friend, a Brahmin, suggested that Mohandas should go to England for studies. His mother was shocked by the idea and only agreed when he took solemn vows not to eat meat or drink wine or to go with women. So he left home to sail for England from Bombay, saying goodbye to Kasturbai, who was nursing their infant son.

In Bombay his plan to study in England ran into strong opposition from the leaders of his caste community. They forbade him to go to England because, according to their religious beliefs, any orthodox Hindu who crossed the sea would lose his caste and become Untouchable because he would be obliged to eat and drink with Europeans.

Mohandas, who was not yet nineteen, showed his courage and independence of spirit; in spite of being declared outcaste by the community he set out for England in September 1888. His elder brother, Laxmidas, had supported him loyally in this dispute. The young man sailing for England was completely unaware of the problems he was going to face. He was not prepared either by education or experience to meet such a new and strange way of life. His own religious beliefs were far from clear and he was already beginning to rebel against some of the more extreme prejudices of Hinduism. What he had, though, was a firm sense of right and wrong, a determined character and a strong attachment to the truth.

The India which Mohandas left behind was the most important and complicated region of the British Empire. Although many of the states were nominally ruled by their own princes, the greater part of the population, in the most important provinces, were firmly ruled by governors and officials appointed by the British Crown. Even the princely states were severely limited in their powers.

The provinces and states of India varied in their languages and traditions just as they do today. They were different also in their people and in their geography. The prosperous and fertile Punjab, with its cheerful and energetic people, was very different from Bihar, a state where the population suffers under plague and famine caused by extremes of both flood

opposite: *An artist's impression of a busy street in a small town in Gujarat. In the little shops customers are bargaining for food, for lengths of cotton to make clothes, or for household utensils.*

The British Indian Empire

and drought. The proud Rajputs of the harsh underdeveloped highland plateau were, and are, very different from the highly political Bengalis, living in the great rice plain or in the crowded city of Calcutta.

India was, for most of its long history, divided into areas with different systems of government. Only on three occasions before the establishment of British rule did administrations exist which attempted to unify the continent. These were the empires of Ashoka in 250 BC, of Chandragupta I, some six hundred years later, and of the Moghuls, whose power was only secure during the seventeenth century, and whose greatest administrator was Akbar the Great. These empires in their day were well administered and efficiently governed by strong emperors backed by large armies, trained officials and secret services.

The British Empire, which grew slowly over two hundred years, but openly took charge of all India only in 1858 after the Great Rebellion, was different from all the others in that its strengths and weaknesses did not depend upon one man. It was a huge official organisation that worked like a machine; and this made the men who served in it carry out their duties without much sympathy for the feelings, thoughts and wishes of the Indian people. Though there were many individual district officers who knew and helped to solve the problems of the villagers, the administrators gave the impression of being aloof and distant. While they worked hard and honestly for the country, it seemed that they did not love or really understand the people.

Another aspect of the British administration different from anything which had gone before was its respect for the

The commercial port of Bombay in the 1880s. The churches, warehouses and offices of a great city like Bombay show the influence of European styles of building.

principle of personal liberty under laws that treated everybody the same, no matter how they varied in religion or caste or race. In all this, as in many other matters, it may be fairly said of the British that they considered peoples' welfare rather than their feelings. The cleverest young men from Oxford and Cambridge, conscious of their duty and very sure of themselves, came out to govern India. They often irritated growing numbers of educated Indians. At the same time they maintained peace and order. They encouraged more efficient agriculture, introduced modern European industry and communications and made millions of Indians more prosperous.

Held by a firm administration, India, for the first time in history, began to work as one country, and Indians, for the first time, began to think of themselves as Indians, instead of simply as Rajputs or Bengalis, for example. Had this not been so, it is unlikely that Mohandas Gandhi and men like him could have risen to the leadership of this vast and varied continent.

On the other hand, had India not produced, during its long history, some of the great saints and religious teachers of mankind, holy men with traditions of self-sacrifice and the rejection of worldly wealth, it is impossible to think that a man like Mohandas could become her greatest leader in modern times.

2 Mohandas in England

Mohandas says this of his first few days in London: 'I would continually think of my home and my country. It was impossible to share my misery with anyone. Everything was strange – the people, their ways of life and even their houses.'

In spite of the strangeness and his homesickness he tried in all kinds of ways to conform to what he thought was expected of him. He began to wear the most expensive and fashionable Bond Street clothes. In February 1890 a friend who met Mohandas in Piccadilly Circus wrote an amusing description of his appearance.

'He was wearing a high silk top hat, polished bright, a stiff starched collar, a flashy tie of all the colours of the rainbow under which was a fine striped silk shirt. He wore a morning coat, a double breasted waist coat and dark striped trousers. He had leather gloves and a silver topped cane and was at the very height of fashion for a young man about town.'

The Strand, 1890, looking east towards St Mary le Strand.

above: *The lobby and main staircase of the Hotel Victoria in 1890, a fashionable and expensive hotel near Trafalgar Square. Gandhi stayed here for his first few days in England, before the expense became too great and he had to move.*

right: *A wedding in St Paul's Cathedral, 1883. Compare this with the Hindu wedding on page 7.*

Life in London at this time reached a high point of gaiety and excitement. The music-halls, the theatres and the fashionable cafes were full of elegantly dressed men and women. Horse-buses, cabs and carriages and crowds of pedestrians produced the appearance of busy chaos, of energy and liveliness. England was powerful and confident.

Mohandas learned that to be a proper English gentleman he must be able to dance and speak French. He writes: 'I decided to take dancing lessons and paid down three pounds for a term. I must have taken about six lessons in three weeks. It was beyond me to achieve anything like a rhythmic motion. I could not follow the piano and found it impossible to keep time.' He also bought a violin and scratched away on it for a week or two trying to form an appreciation of Western music. After some time he realised that fiddling and dancing would not make a gentleman of him, but that being a gentleman was really a matter of good character and honourable behaviour. So he began to devote himself to study for the London Matriculation and to prepare himself for Law School. He read the newspapers eagerly and joined a vegetarian society, becoming a member of the committee. He never overcame his shyness in London, however,

above: *Gandhi photographed when he was a law student in London.*

right: *Baron's Court Road W14 about 1900. Gandhi lived at No. 20. He paid 30 shillings a week (£1.50) for bed and board. Finding that too expensive he moved to Tavistock Street, WC1, where his total expenses were 15 shillings a week.*

and was always embarrassed in a group of people.

It was during this time in London that he first read the *Bhagavad Gita*. A passage in the second chapter impressed him deeply: 'The man who foresakes all desires and puts aside all pride of possession and pride in himself reaches the goal of supreme peace.' In later life Mohandas studied every word of the *Bhagavad Gita* and knew it all by heart. He also read in England a life of the Buddha, *The Light of Asia* by Sir Edwin Arnold. He started to study the Bible and went sometimes to church to listen to the sermons. Of all the passages of the New Testament it was the Sermon on the Mount which most affected him because of the light it shed on the character of Jesus. He carried the words of the Sermon in his heart throughout his life.

'Blessed are the poor in spirit: for theirs is the kingdom of heaven.

Blessed are they that mourn: for they shall be comforted.

Blessed are the meek: for they shall inherit the earth.

Blessed are they which do hunger and thirst after righteousness: for they shall be filled.

Blessed are the merciful: for they shall obtain mercy.

Blessed are the pure in heart: for they shall see God.

Blessed are the peacemakers: for they shall be called the children of God.

Love your enemies, bless them that curse you, do good to them that hate you, and pray for them which despitefully use you, and persecute you.'

below: *A trial at the Old Bailey in late Victorian times. The prisoners are in the dock on the left, faced by the judge. The jury are seated at the back and beside them stands the witness giving evidence. In the foreground are the lawyers and in the well of the court, the clerks.*

Mohandas lived a hard and lonely life in London. He was often hungry because of the difficulty in finding the sort of food he could eat. He had few friends, not because he was unfriendly, but because of the strains that this strange life separated from his family imposed upon him. He was always thinking of India, of the bright sun, the colour, the almost daily festivals. He missed the love of his family and the security of living among his own people leading their simple, unhurried and traditional lives.

In June 1891 he passed his Law Examinations at the Inner Temple, one of the Inns of Court in London, was enrolled as a lawyer and prepared to return to India immediately.

On his arrival in Bombay, Laxmidas met him and broke the news that his mother had died only a few weeks before. His family had decided not to tell him while he was studying in case he might fail the examinations. Mohandas received the news calmly though his grief was too deep for tears. He had worshipped his mother and he had been her favourite son.

3 Failure in India

Mohandas found himself something of a stranger in the little town of Rajkot to which he returned. His family was no longer influential, and their hopes that Mohandas would succeed his father in the appointment of Dewan were not realised. Much money had been spent on sending him to England and it was necessary to find a job. Lawyers were not in short supply in India, and there was no opportunity for him to build up a legal practice in Rajkot. He applied for a school-teaching job but was not considered qualified for it.

On his return to India the caste community insisted that he should undergo ceremonial purification and penance, so he went to bathe in the holy Godavari River to wash away the sins they thought he must have committed in England. Returning to Rajkot he gave a meal in honour of the elders of his caste and, stripped to the waist, he served humbly at the tables. Underneath he was boiling with anger at the indignities brought upon him by their stupid superstitions.

His treatment of his wife Kasturbai at this time was unkind. He wanted everything changed to suit his newly acquired Western ideas and he insisted that she should take up reading and writing and learn English social graces. Kasturbai was a simple, homely girl but she had enough spirit to resist being changed against her will. Mohandas had temporarily lost his direction and his overbearing behaviour was the result of this uncertainty. Unfortunately, it was typical of many young Indian men who had obtained superficial training in England and then returned to lord it over their families whom they now saw as ignorant and backward. They felt ashamed of their own people.

Pilgrims praying and bathing in the River Ganges. The brass pots are for carrying away the sacred water of the river.

Published from 1838. 'The Times of India' was one of the first newspapers to cater for the British living in India and for the English-speaking Indian middle-class, whose numbers increased rapidly towards the end of the nineteenth century. These Indians now began to take a greater part in serving and advising the British administration.

Although the affairs of the little backwater state of Rajkot had not changed much since Mohandas had gone away to England, India itself was undergoing important political and social changes. The universities of Calcutta, Delhi and Madras were producing large numbers of young men ambitious to take part in the leadership of society. Whether they had studied literature, law or medicine they had also read the works of English political philosophers and reformers. There was an increasing number of newspapers and journals to inform a growing and politically conscious middle class. Modernisation, such as the provision of railways, telegraph and improved sanitation, and the growth of commerce, was making the towns and cities more prosperous and local self-government was starting in these urban communities.

The Indian National Congress had been founded in 1885 with small numbers and limited political objectives. It held annual conferences in different large cities in turn and it was not long before it had a large membership and many sympathisers devoted to the cause of a democratic India. The Muslim minority, which for some years after the Great Rebellion of 1857–8 had been inactive in education and politics, began to come to life again with the foundation of an Anglo-Arabic College in 1875. This college was later to become the Muslim University of Aligarh, the source and inspiration of Muslim social and political advance. (As time went on, the Congress began to be identified with the Hindu majority and later, in 1906, the Muslim league was founded to maintain the influence of the Muslims.)

The railway system of India was built in the last half of the nineteenth century. Masses of Indian labourers with the help of British engineers overcame many difficulties to make the most extensive railway network in the world.

So, already, when Mohandas was wondering what to do for a living in Rajkot, the great movements and divisions of modern Indian history were beginning to take shape.

For a short while Mohandas went to Bombay to look for work in the courts. He writes of his first case: 'I appeared for the defendant and had to cross-examine the plaintiff's witnesses. I stood up but my heart sank into my boots. My head was reeling and I felt as if the whole court was doing likewise. I could think of no questions to ask. The judge must have laughed and the other lawyers, no doubt, enjoyed the spectacle.' He sat down in confusion and after returning the fee of thirty rupees to his disappointed client he rushed out of the court. After this he returned to Rajkot and made a modest living writing petitions for the simple folk who could neither write properly nor understand the law.

When he and Kasturbai were together again they began to lead a more harmonious life and soon a second son, Manilal, was born to them. However, Mohandas was not able to retrieve the sinking fortunes of his family, and he began to feel that if he were to make a success of his profession he would have to do so abroad. But how?

Just at this moment, a Muslim merchant in Porbandar who had business connections in South Africa offered him a year's contract to undertake some legal work in Durban. The fee offered was £105 and all his living and travelling expenses. Of course the offer was accepted and Mohandas gave all the money to Laxmidas, who would be responsible for looking after Kasturbai and the children. He left for Durban in May 1893.

4 Conflict in South Africa

The South Africa to which Mohandas went was to change very considerably during the twenty years he stayed.

When he arrived the country consisted of the British colonies of Natal and Cape Colony, and also of two self-governing territories occupied by Boer settlers of Dutch descent, Transvaal and the Orange Free State. The two groups of Europeans had never coexisted easily, but by now the Boers, with some reason, deeply distrusted the British, whom they suspected of coveting the wealth of their land, and of wanting control over the entire country. So it came as little surprise when war broke out between the two in 1899, ending with victory for the British in 1902. Nearly all the Boers' losses, including virtual self-government, had been made good by 1906 – 'They gave us back our country in everything but name' was the comment of Jan Smuts, one of their leaders – and in 1910 the four states combined voluntarily to form the Union of South Africa, a self-governing member of the British Empire. But many Boers resented their loss of independence, and never really liked the arrangement.

This conflict, however, was not the only one between sections of the population; nor, for Gandhi, was it the most important. By the 1890s the population of the area included about 2,000,000 Africans, 750,000 Europeans, and 75,000 Indians. The Indians had begun to arrive thirty years before, as contract labourers to work the sugar plantations of Natal. In fact it was characteristic of the British Empire, in Africa and elsewhere, that much of the labour force was drawn from the population of India. Having fulfilled their five-year contracts, in conditions of near-slavery, many Indian workers decided to stay in the country, where they were joined by their families. Later, gradually, merchants and more professional people from India came out to make a living in these growing communities.

As the Indian communities grew in size and commercial importance, the Europeans began to see them as a political

South Africa, about 1900

threat which they sought increasingly to control. When Natal and Cape Colony were granted internal self-government their governments began to encroach on the freedom of the Indians, who lost the right to vote. It became almost impossible for Indians to obtain trading licences. Residence and registration requirements made it difficult for them to move about the country. The government also attempted to restrict immigration and white mobs tried to stop Indians from landing at Durban docks. Eventually it was the government of British India which intervened. In 1904, after the Orange Free State had already banned Indian immigration, they refused to allow emigration to the Transvaal gold mines and in 1911 prohibited

above: *Indian women picking tea on a plantation in Natal in the 1890s.*

right: *Indian men cutting sugar cane in the 1890s.*

Indians from travelling to Natal. The government in England did express concern for the Indians in South Africa, and tried to restrain the colonial government. But in England this was not a matter that worried many people. Anyway, having granted self-government to colonies, the British government could no longer direct their internal affairs. In all these issues, and especially in the struggles of the Indian community in South Africa, Mohandas became increasingly involved.

When he docked at Durban the merchant from Porbandar was there to meet him, and after a day or two he took Mohandas to the court to see how things were done. Mohandas was wearing a black turban which the magistrate ordered him to remove. But, as there were other Indians there wearing turbans, he refused and left the courtroom. He then wrote to a newspaper explaining his action. This started a fierce

Pietermaritzburg station in the 1880s.

correspondence, bringing him to the attention of the Indians in Durban.

There was little work for Mohandas in Durban as his firm's work was in the hands of an experienced man, so for his first case he was sent to Pretoria to represent his employer in a lawsuit. He studied the case in great detail before setting off. He was given first class tickets and the company's agents along the route were told of his coming and instructed to look after his needs.

On the way, at Pietermaritzburg a European man entered the carriage, saw an Indian sitting there and went away to complain. A railway official arrived and ordered Mohandas into a third class carriage. He showed his first class ticket and refused to budge. In spite of this a policeman was called and Mohandas was thrown out of the carriage with his baggage and left on the platform. He went to sit in the dark and deserted waiting room all through the long and chilly night. While he sat there, he thought deeply. He had never had such an experience before. He was very angry and almost made up his mind to return to Durban and to leave South Africa for ever. He then remembered his duty to his employer and decided to stick it out. Another and more important reason occurred to him. The ill-treatment he had received was the result of the madness of colour prejudice. It was his duty to do everything in his power to destroy it.

In his book *Satyagraha in South Africa* he recalls his feelings:

'I should try if possible to root out the disease of colour prejudice and suffer hardships in the process. I experienced further insults and received more beatings on my way to Pretoria but this only confirmed me in my determination.' Many years later in India, when Mohandas was asked to recall the most significant experience in his political life, he told the story of his night on the station at Pietermaritzburg.

From Charlestown on the border of Natal Province Mohandas had to go by coach to Johannesburg. This was a journey of great difficulty and he saw and felt for himself the indignities suffered by coloured people who were not allowed inside the coach. The Dutch coachman tried to make him sit on the floor on some sacking instead of on a seat and when Mohandas refused he was beaten up. At Johannesburg he tried to book a room in a hotel but was refused. On the following morning he booked a first class ticket to Pretoria. At one of the stations on the way a guard told him to go to a third class carriage and Mohandas felt his heart sinking once again. This time, however, an Englishman in the carriage warned the guard and Mohandas remained. Finally he arrived in Pretoria much affected by the journey and pondering deeply about what should be the weapon with which to destroy colour prejudice.

He decided that the weapon should be truth and invented the name *Satyagraha* for it. *Satya* is a Sanskrit word meaning 'truth' and *agraha* means 'force', so Satyagraha can be approximately translated as 'Truth Weapon'. Mohandas later described the Truth Weapon as 'the vindication of truth not by inflicting suffering on the opponent but on oneself. The opponent is to be weaned away from error by patience and sympathy.'

This weapon, which Mohandas was to use in South Africa and later in India, was forged not only from his own experiences but from his devotion to the *Bhagavad Gita* and to the Sermon on the Mount. 'Love your enemies, bless them that curse you.'

After he had been in Pretoria for only a few days, Mohandas called a public meeting of Indians to tell them how they could improve their conditions. He was then only twenty-four. His absolute conviction of the truth of what he was saying fired his speech and removed all traces of nervousness. It was his first successful public appearance. He told his audience that they should observe honesty and truthfulness in business; cultivate a greater degree of social and personal hygiene (for Europeans thought some of their habits dirty); forget their own rivalries and the divisions between Hindus, Muslims, Parsees and Christians; and learn English.

The lawsuit which Mohandas had come to conduct ended successfully and a farewell party was given in his honour. At the party he was shown a copy of a newspaper which reported plans to take away voting rights from Indians in Natal Province. Mohandas said that the Indians must at once organise a committee to represent their case to the government of the colony. Throughout June 1894 he was busy in Durban organising and speaking at meetings and cultivating powerful friends. Among these were the British Attorney General of Natal and Dada Bai Naoroji, a wealthy Indian in London who had become a member of the British Parliament. At the end of June, Mohandas submitted a well-argued petition to the Natal Assembly declaring the rights of Indians to vote, though without success. He also helped to establish the Natal Indian Congress to channel the social and political activity of the local Indians. Although he had not joined the Indian National Congress at this time he had a great respect for it and wanted the name to be popularised in South Africa. In August 1894 he became secretary of the Natal Congress.

About this time his application for membership of the Supreme Court of Natal as advocate was accepted by the Chief Justice, though opposed by many European lawyers because he was an Indian and coloured. He led an increasingly busy life and was frequently exhausted in mind and body. On one occasion, in search of rest and peace, he visited a Christian missionary community in Zululand. Here the tall, fine-looking Zulus, about a thousand of them, men and women, were being taught farming and other useful crafts and trades by the monks and nuns. He was impressed by the atmosphere of prayer, happiness and progress and at the back of his mind grew the seed of an idea that one day he would found such a community himself.

Early in 1896 he decided that he must go home, not only to see to his family affairs but also to enlist support in India for his campaign for Truth in South Africa. On the ship he wrote a pamphlet calling attention to the grievances of Indians in South Africa and had it printed and published when he reached home in Rajkot. His homecoming was not a rest, however, and he was soon on his travels again, visiting many important men in India, including leaders of the Congress. In November he was recalled to South Africa because of political developments there and he set off, this time with Kasturbai and his two sons.

Some European opponents gathered in Durban in order to give Mohandas and the other Indian passengers, immigrants, a hot reception. He had to be rescued by the police from a hostile mob and sheltered in a police station for two or three days, disguised as an Indian constable. When things became calm again Mohandas found that his position had changed. He was now regarded as the chief political representative of Indians in South Africa, speaking in the name of the most influential leaders in India itself. His social work, his legal cases, his family and even his personal search for God had to wait while he devoted his energies to the political struggle. At the time this centred round the Natal government's determination to stop the immigration of Indian labourers, and begin deporting those who were already there, and meanwhile to make life difficult for Indian merchants, clerks and labourers.

A contemporary engraving from 'Le Petit Journal', a French illustrated newspaper, showing Indian stretcher bearers working alongside the British Medical Corps during the Boer War in 1899.

In October 1899 the Boer War broke out and Mohandas was anxious that the Indians should demonstrate their loyalty to the government. He suggested the formation of a corps of stretcher bearers. This was at first refused, but as things became more difficult for the British his offer was accepted. During the war Mohandas noticed the good qualities of the British soldier and his comradely behaviour towards the Indians. He spoke of it later:

'Tommy was then altogether lovable. He mixed with us freely. He often shared with us his luxuries, if there were

Gandhi (second from right) about the time of his arrest in connection with the 1913 strike. On his left is his secretary, Miss Seblesem, and on is right is a co-worker, H. Kallenbach.

any to be had. Water was very scarce. On one occasion there was only one well and the soldiers who were helping themselves to water at once cheerfully shared their small ration with our bearers. There was a spirit of brotherhood irrespective of colour or creed.'

The Indians behaved very bravely in the war and Mohandas himself carried wounded on stretchers.

When Queen Victoria, Empress of India, died in 1901, millions of Indians mourned her passing. Mohandas sent a telegram of sympathy to London on behalf of the South African Indians and led a mourning procession through the streets of Durban.

This spirit of co-operation unfortunately did not last, and Indians continued to be treated as inferiors in South Africa. In 1907 an Act was passed requiring Indians to carry registration certificates and residence permits. It was at this time that Satyagraha, the Truth Weapon, was first used; Mohandas persuaded many Indians not to register. In January 1908 he was taken before a magistrate and sentenced to two months' imprisonment in Johannesburg, where he was staying at the time. Soon he was joined by 2500 other 'Satyagrahis'. The wives and children of the Indians were looked after on a settlement of a thousand acres given for them to use by a wealthy German Jewish businessman. Mohandas called it Tolstoy Farm, in honour of the great Russian writer whose book *The Kingdom of God is Within You* he so much admired. Tolstoy had written that truly Christian men, acting in pursuit of Truth and Justice, could shake the power of unjust governments. He defined a Christian as a man 'who enters into no dispute with his neighbour, he neither attacks nor uses violence. On the contrary, he suffers himself without resistance and by his very attitude towards evil not only sets himself free but helps to free the world at large from all outward authority.'

In 1909 Mohandas made a visit to England to enlist support there. He believed that if the way Indians were treated in South Africa was widely known, not only in India but in England also, it would become an important issue among British politicians. In this he succeeded, and the plight of the Indians in South Africa could no longer be 'swept under the carpet' by British governments.

After the Union of South Africa was established, with General Botha as Prime Minister, the Europeans in South Africa continued to force through the Union Assembly measures unfavourable to Indians. Special taxes and the ban on immigration continued. A further attack on their rights was made when the Supreme Court ruled in 1913 that only Christian

Gandhi with his pilgrim's staff during the Satyagraha struggle in 1914.

General Smuts in 1914. A general in the First World War, he became Prime Minister of the Union of South Africa in 1919 and again in 1939.

Kasturbai Gandhi in 1915.

marriages were valid. Hindu, Muslim and Parsee marriages became, by a stroke of the pen, invalid. Kasturbai hearing the news reacted with horror – 'Then I am not your wife?' – and she with many other Indian women joined the Satyagrahis. In the same year strikes were organised among Indian industrial and mine workers and many men and women were imprisoned. The government acted harshly and in some places strikers were shot and killed. Tens of thousands of Indians were on strike or in jail but they did not resist arrest or fight against their oppressors. Mohandas too was in prison. In 1913 he was released and in the next year was summoned to have talks with General Smuts. By this time Mohandas had won the support of many reasonable and influential men in South Africa, India and England, by his arguments and the force of his honesty. Smuts too was persuaded, and as a result of their talks an Indian Relief Bill was passed through the Union Parliament in July 1914. Under its provisions most of the regulations passed in recent years against Indians were removed.

Mohandas called the Relief Bill 'the Magna Carta of South African Indians'. It had admitted the principle of racial equality and had proved the strength of the Truth Weapon. In July 1914, Mohandas and Kasturbai set out for England. Before leaving he presented Smuts with a pair of sandals that he had made in prison. Smuts wore them for many years and when in 1939 he returned them to Mohandas as a gesture of friendship he wrote: 'I have worn these sandals for many summers since then even though I feel I am not worthy to stand in the shoes of so great a man.' In the same year Smuts wrote about Mohandas: 'It was my fate to be the opponent of a man for whom even then I had the highest respect. He never lost his temper or succumbed to hate and preserved his gentle humour in the most trying situations.'

So the Truth Weapon had been tried and tested, and Mohandas had made some gains through honesty and gentleness for the Indians in South Africa. It was now to be turned to the great task of liberating India.

5 Mohandas returns to India

During his long stay in South Africa Mohandas had not turned his back upon the problems of India but had written frequently about the ideal of independence.

In 1905 in *Indian Opinion* he had written:

'It is impossible that national aspirations can be forever suppressed and equally impossible for India to remain a "dependency" in an Empire to which it contributes more than half the population. Is it possible for the patriotic spirits of a people with the glorious traditions of India to be content with serfdom? No people exists that would not think itself happier under its own bad government than it might really be under the good government of an alien power.'

At about this time also he wrote a book *Hind Swaraj* (Indian Self-Government) expounding his philosophy of government and explaining the cause of Indian Independence.

On his return to India in 1915 he was already a national figure and widely recognised as a person with great spiritual gifts. Enthusiastic audiences at public meetings began to call out to him 'Mahatmaji! Mahatmaji!' Rabindranath Tagore, India's greatest living writer and Nobel Prizewinner, called Mohandas 'a great soul in peasant's garb' and so the name *Mahatma* (Great Soul) was conferred upon him at this time. But he was never comfortable with this or any other honour which might put him above the simple folk of India. The Mahatma and Tagore were both great lovers of India but in different ways. Once Gandhi told Tagore the poet: 'The suffering millions need only one poem – food'.

Tagore, while he worked to advance the cause of Indian culture, accepted the benefits of the modernisation which the West had brought. The Mahatma looked always to the glories of India's past, to the golden age of God-King Rama's rule. He wished to resist the influences of Western industrialisation which, he believed, in the end could only bring misery to the people. The Mahatma was essentially a reformer of Hinduism, urging the people to throw off the superstitions and cruelties of their corrupt and caste-ridden society and to become new, free men by returning to the old pure principles of their faith. He wanted them, above all, to put the principles of the *Bhagavad Gita* into practice in their everyday lives. He believed that the chains which bound India were made by India herself. In *Hind Swaraj* he wrote: 'Some Englishmen say that they took and hold India by the sword. This is wrong. We alone keep them; we strengthen their hold by quarrelling among ourselves.'

In his attitude to independence the Mahatma often found himself in conflict with other groups in India. One of these was revolutionary and wanted to expel the British by armed force. The other was the Indian National Congress, led mainly by the English-educated upper classes, lawyers and officials. The Congress wanted self-government eventually, for a Westernised and industrial India. The Mahatma was not so much interested in *who* ruled India as in *how* India was ruled. While the Congress had nothing to say about the peasants, who formed the vast majority of the population, because it did not know them, Gandhi was concerned with them above all. At the opening of the Benares Hindu University in 1916 the Mahatma said: 'Our salvation can only come through the peasant. Neither the doctors nor the lawyers nor the rich landlords are going to secure it.' He tried to show that lifting the burden of poverty and ignorance from the bent shoulders of hundreds of millions of Indian peasants could not be done as the result of the arguments of a small group of Westernised lawyers and businessmen, nor could it be the gift of a foreign power. Their political freedom could only be achieved by themselves having first won freedom for their souls. The Mahatma was essentially a religious teacher.

The centre of his religious activity at this time was the *ashram*, or monastery, which he founded in 1915 in Ahmedabad

Gandhi founded many ashrams. From 1935 to 1945 he lived in a hut (right) in the ashram at Sevagram Wardha near Nagpur in Central India. His room has been kept unaltered. The few things show the simplicity of the Mahatma's life.

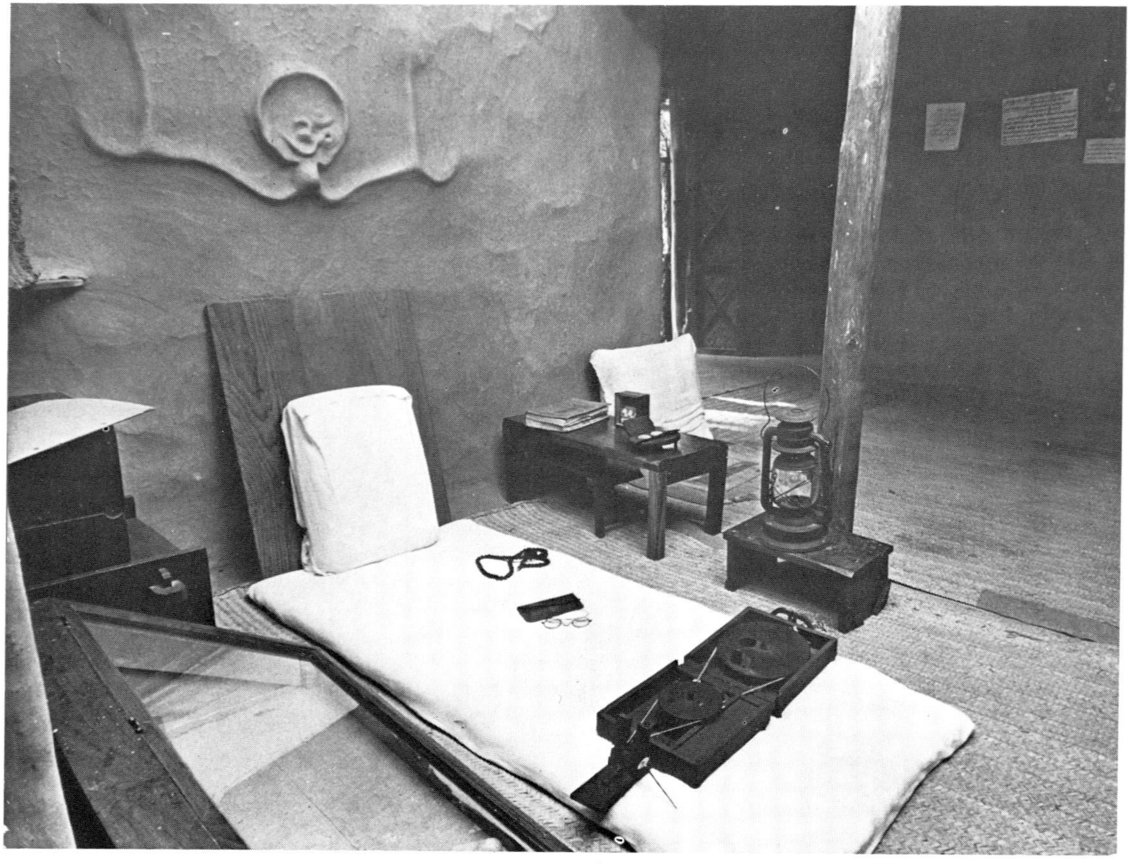

A street sweeper is an Untouchable, for his job would be considered defiling by a Hindu of any caste.

in Gujarat. He called it Satyagraha Ashram. His followers, numbering at different times between fifty and two hundred disciples, led a simple life of prayer, study, manual work and helping the local people. In a group of small whitewashed huts, standing in a grove of shady trees near the river, the Mahatma lived in a little cell teaching any who cared to listen. Many of the most influential leaders of the independence movement came, like disciples, to sit at his feet. He did not confine himself to prayer and preaching, however, but in the next few years went out, and by train and on foot visited every part of India.

Very soon what the Mahatma preached about the equality of all men was to be put to the test in Satyagraha Ashram. In India there were, and still are, tens of millions of Untouchables. The Untouchables are completely outside the caste system of Hinduism, rejected outcasts whose social conditions are the most degraded in the world. They live in slums and are confined to the demeaning tasks of removing human excrement, dead animals and human corpses. High caste Hindus consider themselves polluted if Untouchables use the same wells, enter the temples, or even if the shadow of an Untouchable falls across them. The Mahatma called them *Harijans* (children of God) and devoted himself to raising them up to human dignity.

An Untouchable family wanted to join the ashram and the Mahatma accepted them. The financial help he had been receiving from a wealthy caste Hindu stopped immediately and threats were made by others to boycott the ashram and drive its members away. Other Hindus, however, continued to support it, and the Mahatma carried on his campaign for the Untouchables. On one occasion he wrote in the magazine *Young India*.

'Hinduism has sinned in giving support to Untouchability. It has degraded us and made us the outcasts of the British Empire. The crimes for which we condemn the British Government we have been guilty of ourselves towards our Untouchable brothers. It is useless to talk of Swaraj so long as we do not protect the weak and the helpless.'

The Mahatma's political activities at this time were devoted to helping Congress, by making speeches and attending conferences, but most of all by being its conscience. In 1917 an opportunity occurred for him to use the Truth Weapon on a large scale in India itself.

In Champaran, an out-of-the-way area in the state of Bihar,

there were many British-owned estates. The peasant farmers were compelled to plant and harvest a proportion of indigo as rent for their lands. Indigo was a plant much used for dyes, but when chemical substitutes were invented there followed a slump in the indigo industry. The landlords immediately increased the rents and added taxes also. These new rents and taxes were collected with police and military assistance, and the peasants were helpless. The Mahatma was invited by one of the farmers, Raj Kumar Shukla, to come to Champaran. As soon as he was able, he went to investigate their grievances. He made hundreds of reports and submitted them to the government. At first there was no response, so the Mahatma organised a strike. The landlords responded brutally by beating up the strikers but the resolution of the peasants held and they did not repay violence with violence. At length the Lieutenant-Governor of Bihar put the Mahatma on a commission to investigate the problem and to suggest solutions. The commission accepted his arguments and made its decision. The landlords were no longer to be permitted to exploit and terrorise the peasants and they were ordered to repay the taxes which they had taken unjustly. After this the Mahatma was looked upon as a liberator. In the face of the violence of the landlords the peasants had triumphed. 'Blessed are the meek: for they shall inherit the earth.' The Mahatma had taught them how to carry out a successful strike.

At about this time he became interested in the possibility of loosening the stranglehold of British factory-made imports by developing Indian village industries. British economic power was exemplified by huge imports into India of cheap cotton cloth made in Lancashire. The Mahatma proposed a policy of *swadeshi* which means 'of the country'. He adapted the spinning wheel and produced a simple machine which could be made and used by the most backward peasants to produce their own cotton cloth. Gradually the movement was taken up by thousands of peasants and the simple cotton cloth called *khadi* became the uniform of the Mahatma's followers. It was also adopted by the leaders of Congress. The wheel, which for the Buddha had been the symbol of the Law, became, for the Mahatma, the symbol of India's independence from foreign commercial power. It now appears on the flag of free India.

The Mahatma saw that his plan for raising up the peasants would make little progress without proper village education. He started the movement by opening six primary schools in the villages in Champaran district in 1917. The teachers, volunteers, were to be paid by the villagers, not in money but in food and accommodation. Because the villages were so dirty and disease-ridden the Mahatma instructed his teachers to concentrate less on grammar and arithmetic and more on cleanliness and good manners.

While he was still at Champaran a letter came to the Mahatma describing the desperate poverty of the workers in the cloth factories at Ahmedabad. He went there and found the mill owners quite friendly, except that they refused to allow the workers' claim for higher wages to be discussed. At this the Mahatma urged the workers to strike and laid down instructions as to how they should do so. He gave four rules:

1. Never resort to violence.
2. Never molest non-strikers.
3. Never beg for food.
4. Never give in.

The strike lasted for twenty-one days. When, towards the end, the hungry strikers showed signs of giving up, the Mahatma told them that if they did not continue, he would fast. In any case he would share their hunger until the strike was successful. The Mahatma fasted for three days. The mill owners gave in and agreed to pay reasonable wages. So another battle had been won with the Truth Weapon. There had been no violence and no hatred and the Mahatma had taken the sufferings of the hungry on himself.

Gandhi spinning, 1925. Gandhi required his followers to spend some of each day spinning. The spinning wheel became a symbol of national self-sufficiency or 'swadeshi'. Gandhi often used his spinning wheel to relax his mind.

A child spinning in a village street. The spinning wheel consists of two sets of wooden spokes joined by criss-crossing strings. These strings support another loop which encircles a spindle which is mounted horizontally, at the opposite end of the frame. When the spinner turns the wheel with her right hand the loop acts as a driving belt and turns the spindle. To spin the cotton fibre into thread the spinner teases out some of the fibre and attaches it to the spindle. At first she holds the cotton horizontally in line with the spindle and turns the wheel to twist the thread. Then she draws her hand back and away, extending the fibres as they are twisted; next she brings her hand up at right angles to the spindle, so that the next turn of the wheel rolls the spun yarn onto the spindle. Then the process is repeated.

6 The parting of the ways

The vast majority of Indian people loyally obeyed the British government throughout the Great 1914–18 War. There were almost a million Indian soldiers fighting for the Empire in Europe, the Middle East and Asia. They did more than their duty, as the number of Victoria Crosses won by the Indian Army testifies. The Mahatma, however much he criticised the government, considered himself a loyal subject of the Crown and used his influence in support of the war effort. He wrote to the Viceroy: 'I would make India offer all her able-bodied sons as a sacrifice to the Empire at this critical moment. I know that India by this very act would become the most favoured partner in the Empire and racial distinctions would become a thing of the past.' When people criticised the Mahatma for supporting the British in war he argued that war was not always evil. In this he seems to have been inconsistent with his customary teaching. He reasoned, no doubt, that self-government would be granted by the British as a reward for India defending the Empire. Meanwhile, when the war began the government introduced the Defence of India Act which made the campaign for self-government illegal.

If the Mahatma, other Indian leaders and the people were hoping after the war for a relaxation of wartime regulations which restricted political activities, the release of independence campaigners from prison and the restoration of civil liberties they were to be disappointed. A commission headed by Mr Justice Rowlatt came from England to study the political situation in India and to recommend measures to the government. In March 1919, far from relaxing emergency regulations, the Rowlatt Act was passed imposing harsh measures to stifle the Independence Movement. It was a great

right: *Indian cavalry going through a French village during World War 1.*

blow to moderate Indian leaders, for there had been many official hints that India would have internal self-government after the war and that a series of long overdue reforms would be introduced. They felt deceived and betrayed.

The Mahatma now launched his Truth Weapon directly against the British government. He decided to call a general strike, or *hartal*, throughout the whole of India for 6 April 1919. It would last for one day, and during that day the Indian people would fast to symbolise the humiliation they suffered from being ruled over by a foreign power. It was an incredible idea: to bring all the shops, factories, offices, farms, railways, and the work of 300 million people to a standstill. The Mahatma himself led the hartal in Bombay. There were outbreaks of violence in some of the large cities such as Delhi, Bombay and Ahmedabad, and lives were lost. Europeans were murdered, public buildings burned and looted, and railways torn up. Crowds, peaceful and violent alike, were charged at by the police swinging heavy, brass-tipped sticks called *lathis*, and hundreds were severely injured. Martial law was declared in several cities. The Mahatma, realising that things had got out of hand, and that violent mobs had taken over from the Satyagrahis, called off the hartal.

The next act in the drama of India's independence struggle took place on 13 April 1919 in Amritsar. It is an irony, in the light of what happened, that in this holy city of the Sikhs the hartal had been conducted peacefully; nevertheless, some British feared that a revolt was being planned. On 12 April General Dyer, the British officer commanding troops in Amritsar, made a proclamation prohibiting meetings and processions. This was read in some parts of the city.

The next day Dyer learned that many people intended to hold a meeting in an open place called the Jallianwalla Bagh. It was surrounded by buildings and had very few proper exits and entrances. The general, with about ninety Gurkha and Baluchi soldiers, and two armoured cars, entered

Brigadier-General R. E. H. Dyer (1864–1927). He and his friends thought that he had acted firmly and prevented a full-scale rebellion, but most people thought he had made a disastrous and cruel mistake.

the square, where a speaker standing on a platform was addressing a huge and peaceful audience. Without giving any warning of his intentions Dyer ordered his troops to fire and the firing lasted for ten minutes. Panic among the crowd, causing some to run towards the troops because there was no escape to the rear, increased the casualties. There were 379 unarmed civilians, including women and children, killed and 1,137 wounded. It was Dyer's intention not just to disperse the crowd but to give an example to the people of what they could expect if they resisted the British government. He even refused to allow people to go to the help of the wounded.

After the massacre the Mahatma was convinced that 'the British government today represents Satanism' and nothing less than the removal of the British and complete self-government could satisfy injured India. 'When a government

The bodies of policemen killed when rioters burned the police station at Chauri Chaura in 1921.

takes up arms against its unarmed subjects then it has forfeited its right to govern. It has admitted that it cannot rule in peace and justice.' The general was not satisfied with his victory over unarmed men and women, however, but continued a reign of terror in Amritsar with public floggings and other methods of brutal repression. As the result of an official enquiry General Dyer was relieved of his command and sent home to England in disgrace. The damage had been done, though. The British government and the Indian people had so divided that there could never be a complete reconciliation. For the rest of his life, on the anniversary of the massacre, the Mahatma fasted.

His immediate answer was the policy of non-co-operation which he proposed at a Muslim conference in Delhi in 1919. All British-made goods were to be boycotted. No one should attend British schools or accept government appointments. A month later the government announced reforms in the administration and the handing over of provincial rule to Indian ministries. Responding generously to this British attempt at reconciliation, the Mahatma called off the policy of non-co-operation and urged Congress to make their best efforts to carry through the reforms. His influence was very great and his advice was accepted. After a year, however, when it was clear that the reforms were not going far or fast enough and that British policy had not fundamentally changed, the Mahatma renewed the policy of non-co-operation. In this he had the support of Muslims as well as Hindus. The professional classes also followed him. Lawyers, among them Jawaharlal Nehru, left the British courts, and students abandoned the universities. Peasants withheld their taxes and more and more people stopped buying British goods. The Mahatma travelled all over India preaching this non-violent campaign.

His insistence on non-violence was so strong and his position in Indian politics so dominant that the Congress at its annual meeting in 1921 adopted his resolution of a non-violent civil disobedience campaign. The British responded with lathi charges against crowds and by imprisoning the leaders of the Independence Movement. By January 1922, 10,000 Indians were in prison for political offences. In spite of the Mahatma's instructions, violence broke out in several places and in one incident in the town of Chauri Chaura, twenty-two policemen were murdered by the mob. He again called off the campaign because he did not want it to succeed by evil means. He said at the time: 'It is better to be charged with cowardice and weakness than to sin against God by denying our oath of non-violence'.

On 10 March 1922 the Mahatma was arrested and charged with sedition, that is with encouraging others to disobey the law. During the trial he explained how he had been transformed from a loyal British subject to a person who found it impossible to co-operate with a government which, even with many good intentions, was slowly making India more wretched and helpless than she ever was in the past. Before pronouncing sentence the judge said that the law was no respecter of persons but that it would be impossible to deny that the Mahatma was a great leader and patriot. 'Even those who do not agree with your politics look upon you as a man of high ideals and of noble and saintly life.' He was then sentenced to six years' imprisonment.

In January 1924 after almost two years in prison the Mahatma became very ill with appendicitis and was taken to the hospital in Poona nearby. A British Army surgeon operated on him. Although the operation was successful his recovery was slow and the authorities released him from prison to recuperate. As soon as he was well enough he began to devote his energies to trying to solve the problem of Hindu–Muslim conflicts. He realised that the future of India lay in solving the problem of the deep disunity between them, equally and naturally, as he said, Sons of India. In September 1924 as a result of a clash between the two communities in the North West Frontier Province the Mahatma, though still not fully recovered, started a three-week fast for unity. He brought himself almost to the point of death but Hindu and Muslim leaders all over India made greater efforts to urge their people to live in peace. During his fast he was nursed by a Christian missionary and cared for in a Muslim house by two Muslim doctors.

For the next few years, during which the Mahatma stayed mostly in his ashram, his principal writings appeared in a magazine called *Young India*. In examining these writings we can obtain clear insights into his character and ideals.

'I live for India's freedom and would die for it because it is a part of Truth.'

'I am not interested in freeing India only from the English yoke but from any yoke whatsoever. Thus for me the movement of Swaraj is a movement of self-purification.'

'My mission is not simply the brotherhood of Indian humanity. My mission is not merely freedom for India. But through the freedom of India I hope to realise and carry on the mission of the Brotherhood of Man.'

'My attitude towards the English is one of friendliness and respect. I have respect for Englishmen because I recognise their bravery, their spirit of sacrifice for what they believe to be good, their sticking together and their powers of organisation. A time will come when England will be glad of India's friendship and India will not refuse to take the hand of England because it has once despoiled her.'

'I hate the exploitation of India just as I hate from the bottom of my heart the hideous system of Untouchability for which millions of Hindus are responsible. But I do not hate Englishmen just as I refuse to hate Hindus. I wish to reform them in all the loving ways that are open to me. My non-co-operation is rooted not in hatred but in love. I cannot love Muslims and Hindus and hate Englishmen. Where there is love there is life. Hatred leads to destruction.'

'My Swaraj will not be the result of the murder of others. I shall work for an India in which there shall be no high class or low class people. An India in which all communities shall live in harmony. There can be no room in such an India for the curse of Untouchability. Women shall enjoy the same rights as men and no one shall be exploited.'

7 The salt tax Satyagraha

In December 1928, the annual meeting of the Indian National Congress was held in Calcutta. The most prominent leaders at this session were Subhas Chandra Bose and Jawaharlal Nehru. Bose, whose war cry was 'Give me blood and I will give you freedom,' gradually moved to an extreme revolutionary position and left Congress. He later founded the Indian National Army in the Second World War, hoping to help the Japanese drive the British out of India. Nehru was a young Cambridge-educated lawyer from Allahabad, of a distinguished and wealthy family. He also argued for 'Independence Now' but was not seeking blood as well. Both men advocated an immediate declaration of independence.

At this time India was seething with political and industrial unrest, and there was terrorism and bombing. The Viceroy, Lord Irwin, later Lord Halifax, was a humane and liberal man devoted to reconciliation. A Labour government sympathetic to India's desire for independence was in power in Britain. The Mahatma was prepared to compromise, against the advice of Nehru and Bose, and to attend a Round Table Conference in London to plan the progress of India towards internal self-government. However, in the meantime the opponents of Indian independence in England had been marshalling their forces. As a result, at an interview with the Mahatma and other Indian leaders, Lord Irwin had to say that he could not promise self-government as a natural result of the Conference, and hopes were again dashed.

At the next session of Congress in Lahore in 1929, at which Nehru presided, the Indian leaders, now with the Mahatma's approval, declared in favour of complete independence and withdrawal from the Empire. Congress members who occupied posts in state legislatures were instructed to withdraw, and the people were told not to pay taxes.

The Mahatma wrote a letter to the Viceroy listing the grievances of the Indian people, especially the tax on salt. He wrote: 'nothing but organised non-violence can check

Gandhi with his followers on their march to the sea, 1930.

the organised violence of the British government'. He warned that if the Viceroy would not negotiate an end to the grievances he would organise a campaign of civil disobedience against the salt tax.

On 12 March 1930, with eighty disciples from his ashram, the Mahatma began the long march to the sea which ended at Dandi twenty-four days later. As they passed through the villages on the way, the Mahatma preached to the villagers who spread leaves on the dusty roads for him to walk on. Many local officials resigned their appointments under the British and thousands of people joined the marching column. Young men and women, students from the towns, came out to support

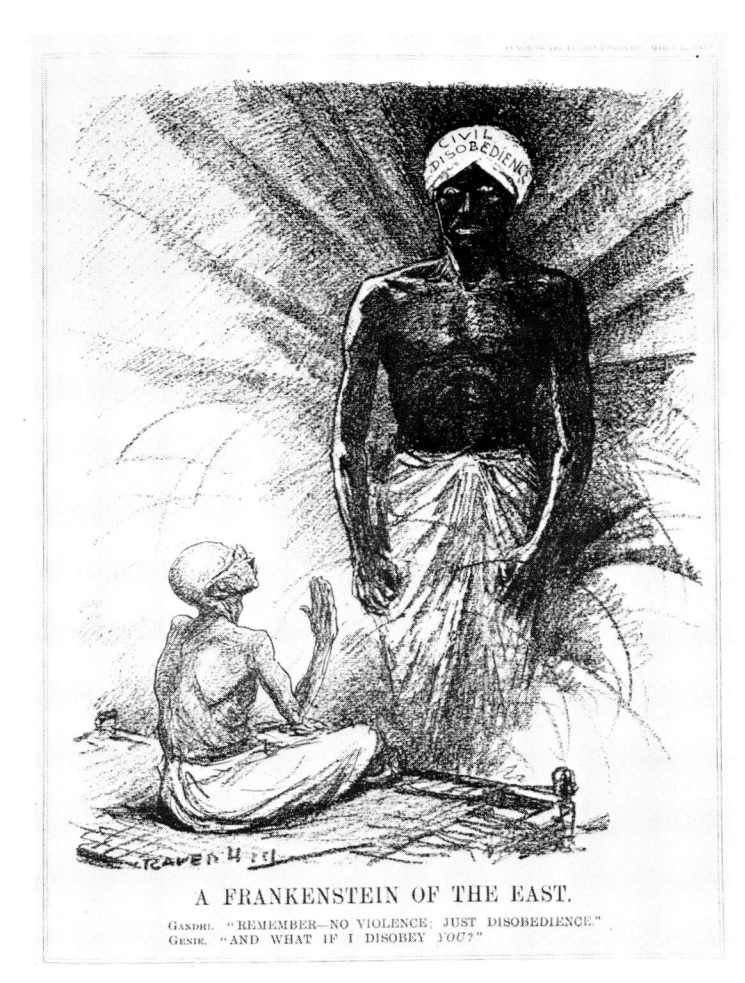

A FRANKENSTEIN OF THE EAST.
GANDHI. "REMEMBER—NO VIOLENCE: JUST DISOBEDIENCE."
GENIE. "AND WHAT IF I DISOBEY YOU?"

On the day the salt march began this cartoon appeared in 'Punch'. Many British thought that Gandhi was a sincere but simple man who did not understand the real world of politics, while some thought that he was stirring up trouble among people who would have been quiet and content. A few thought that he was a hypocrite, greedy for fame.

A compound for habitual prisoners in the Yearavda, near Poona, 6 May 1930. It was crowded with Gandhi's followers, many of whom took their spinning wheels to prison with them.

the Mahatma. 'We are marching in the name of God,' he said.

On 5 April many thousands of people arrived at the seashore. That night they prayed. Next morning they began to collect sea water to evaporate it for the salt. The government monopoly which made it an offence to possess salt which had not been bought from official shops was broken. All along India's thousands of miles of coast people began to make their own salt. The police made thousands of arrests. The Mahatma, Nehru and sixty thousand of their followers were imprisoned. It was a peaceful revolution and the Indians did not respond violently to arrests or to beatings. A column of marchers under Manilal Gandhi, the Mahatma's second son, marched to picket the government salt factory at Dharshana, north of Bombay. Here they were met by police and troops flailing lathis. No one resisted or returned blow for blow.

The salt march and what happened afterwards convinced the Indians that one day they could win their independence. It also convinced many of the British officials that they could not hold India by force.

8 The Round Table Conference, 1931

The first session of the Round Table Conference, attended by Indians nominated by the Viceroy, met in London in December 1930, and came to nothing. All the true leaders of India were in jail. The Prime Minister, Ramsay Macdonald, expressed the wish that Congress should be represented at the next meeting. In India the Viceroy released the Congress leaders and the Mahatma asked for an interview. This was granted on 5 March 1931. In England, Winston Churchill complained that the representative of the King-Emperor was negotiating on equal terms 'with a one-time Inner Temple lawyer now a seditious fakir striding half naked up the steps of the Viceroy's palace.' It was a fact that the Mahatma was the acknowledged leader of India and that he was talking to the Viceroy on equal terms. The two men agreed the 'Delhi Pact'. Prisoners would be freed, the manufacture of salt permitted, civil disobedience would cease. Congress would be represented at the Round Table Conference. No promise was made, however, about eventual independence.

In August 1931 the Mahatma, accompanied by his youngest son Devadas and some friends, set off by sea for London as the representative of India at the Round Table Conference. He based himself for nearly three months at Kingsley Hall in the East End of London and would often visit the ordinary British people in their homes. He was specially popular with the children and was always surrounded by newspaper reporters asking him questions. He was invited to Buckingham Palace to have tea with King George V and Queen Mary, and he wore his Indian peasant's clothes, sandals and a shawl. When a reporter seemed shocked by his informal

right: *Gandhi tried to show that he was a friend of the ordinary people and the poor everywhere. Here he is arriving for a meeting with another famous 'little man', Charlie Chaplin, in the East End of London.*

A typical day's programme from Gandhi's diary, 16 October 1931

1.00 a.m.	Reach Kingsley Hall
1.45 a.m.	Finish the spinning quota of 160 yards
1.50 a.m.	Write up the diary
2.00 a.m. to 3.45 a.m.	Sleep
3.45 a.m. to 5.00 a.m.	Day begins with wash and prayer
5.00 a.m. to 6.00 a.m.	Rest
6.00 a.m. to 7.00 a.m.	Walk and give interview while walking
7.00 a.m. to 8.00 a.m.	Morning ablutions and bath
8.00 a.m. to 8.30 a.m.	Breakfast
8.30 a.m. to 9.15 a.m.	Kingsley Hall to Knightsbridge
9.15 a.m. to 10.45 a.m.	Interview with a journalist, an artist, a Sikh member of the delegation, and a merchant
10.45 a.m. to 11.00 a.m.	To St. James's Palace
11.00 a.m. to 1.00 p.m.	At St. James's (conference)
1.00 p.m. to 2.45 p.m.	Luncheon with American journalists
3.00 p.m. to 5.30 p.m.	With the Mohammedans
5.30 p.m. to 7.00 p.m.	With the Secretary of State for India
7.00 p.m. to 7.30 p.m.	Rush home for prayer and evening meal
8.00 p.m. to 9.10 p.m.	Conference of Temperance Workers. Talk on the drink problem in India
9.10 p.m.	Leave for an engagement with the Nawab of Bhopal
9.45 p.m. to Midnight	With the Nawab of Bhopal

above: *The second session of the Round Table Conference. Gandhi can be seen in the middle of the picture. To his right are Lord Sankey and Sir Samuel Hoare.*

right: *Gandhi attracted large, curious and friendly crowds wherever he went during his stay in England. This cheerful reception was in Lancashire.*

dress, and asked if he thought he had enough on, the Mahatma answered, smiling, 'The King was wearing enough for both of us.'

He had talks and meetings with many politicians and people in public life, and thoroughly enjoyed himself. His wit, humour and gentleness, and the purity and sincerity of his character made a great impression on everyone he met. He spoke at several public meetings of his dream of independent India. In Lancashire, the centre of Britain's cotton industry, where his swadeshi policies for cloth-making in India had been one of the causes of great unemployment, he spoke to some of the unemployed. He was received with great affection even here, and the mill-workers and their wives came out to cheer him.

The conference did not succeed because the British, while making it clear that they were prepared to give in to Indian opinion on a federal system of internal self-government, insisted that ultimate independence, including defence and foreign affairs, was not negotiable. There were also difficulties in agreeing what representation in any Indian Parliament should be granted to the Muslims and the Harijans.

A National government, with greater Conservative representation, took over in Britain in November 1931 and this was reflected in the policies in India of the new Viceroy, Lord Willingdon, who believed that a firm hand would break the power of Congress. So, only a week after his return to India in late December, the Mahatma once again found himself in jail. He was accompanied by all the other leaders of Congress. It was apparent that a large number of British political leaders were against granting independence to India now or at any time in the future, because they saw that India was the key to Britain's continuing power in the world.

9 The campaign for the Harijans

In prison again, the Mahatma pursued his calm routines. He often used to say how much he enjoyed the freedom which prison gave him. He spent many hours in prayer and in reading or at his spinning wheel. In January 1932, the first month of his imprisonment, the government carried out a campaign against the leaders of Congress and 35,000 were arrested. Political liberty had ceased to exist in British India.

At the Round Table Conference the disabilities of the Untouchables, the Harijans, had been discussed and a proposal was made to give them separate representation in the legislative assemblies of the Indian states. The Mahatma was against the principle of separating their representation from that of the main community of Hindus because he knew this would only confirm the Harijans' separation from the rest of society. He wrote a letter warning the authorities that if separate Harijan representation were insisted upon, he would fast to death. The authorities replied that no firm decision had been taken and for the time being the matter rested.

Meanwhile, still in prison, the Mahatma experienced the sadness of a final break in his relationship with his first son Harilal. Harilal had been a Satyagrahi in South Africa but had gradually drifted apart from his father. The beginning of their difference, no doubt, was the Mahatma's stubborn refusal to let any of his sons have a proper professional education. He thought they should be simply educated, and not on Western lines. Another cause of the break was the overbearing attitude the Mahatma often adopted to the boys and their mother. It must be admitted that he was not always a considerate father and husband, and that frequently he carried out his experiments in his own family without thinking of their happiness or of what they wanted. Harilal had become a Muslim, though not a sincere one, and had taken up heavy drinking and loose living. He wrote unkind letters to the Mahatma in prison and the breach between them was never healed.

In August 1932 Ramsay MacDonald, the Prime Minister of Britain, announced separate representation for Untouchables. The next day the Mahatma wrote to MacDonald saying that he would start his fast to death on 20 September. MacDonald wrote a courteous reply saying that the measure was designed to help the Untouchables and not to discriminate against them. The Mahatma replied that it was Hinduism itself which was at stake if, by the means of separate electorates, Untouchability were to continue. Jawaharlal Nehru, himself in prison in Dehra Dun, disapproved of the Mahatma's intention to fast but, after receiving a telegram from him, Nehru grudgingly gave his approval.

The Mahatma's fast was not against the British, but to shake the rigid attitude of caste Hindus. 'What I want, what I am living for and what I should be pleased to die for is the removal of Untouchability root and branch.'

He was now more than sixty, and people feared for his life. The prison officials gave as much help as possible to the comings and goings of the Indian leaders who were trying to produce a solution to the problem of Untouchable representation. The Harijan leader, Dr Ambedkar, was offered terms by the Hindu leaders, including the abolition of the status of Untouchability in any future constitution of India. While these discussions were going on in the prison office, all over India, for the first time in history, Untouchables were being welcomed into Hindu temples. Meanwhile the Mahatma was getting weaker and the authorities released Kasturbai, who was also in prison, and allowed her to visit him.

By 26 September the arrangements agreed by Dr Ambedkar and the others were agreed also by the Prime Minister in London. Next day the Mahatma was shown a copy of the agreement and decided to end his fast. The Mahatma had shaken the Hindus, but only for a while. The politicians had come to a compromise, but a few days after the fast ended the Hindus once more closed their temple doors against Harijans.

10 War and independence

When the Second World War started in Europe in 1939, Britain took India into the conflict without consulting the Congress leaders. There was much anger in India at this tactlessness. Nevertheless the Mahatma went immediately to see the Viceroy at Simla. He expressed his belief that Hitler, the German leader, was responsible for the war, and his sympathy for Britain and France.

In 1940 he declared that he wanted to see England neither defeated nor humiliated, and spoke of his confidence in the courage of the British people. Nehru also wanted the British to win the war. The Mahatma knew perfectly well that if Germany with, later, Japan won the war and drove the British out of India, then independence would be impossible to achieve except by an armed struggle and terrible bloodshed. He understood the character of the British well enough to believe that of all the imperial powers they were most likely to yield ultimately to the Truth Weapon. But although the Mahatma approved the British effort against tyranny in other parts of the world, he did not find himself able in conscience to support the war actively, because he had seen little indication that fighting for Britain would bring India's independence any nearer.

Few of the Congress leaders were as much committed to non-violence as he was, however, and in 1940 they agreed to support the British actively if in return they could have immediate independence. The British responded by offering dominion status, that is, internal self-government, immediately the war was won. Nehru now emerged as the leader of Congress. In England Winston Churchill, the Mahatma's old enemy, was Prime Minister and he said of himself, 'I have not become the King's first minister in order to preside over the liquidation of the Empire.'

As a result of the failure of Congress to achieve their aim of independence at once, they turned again to the Mahatma for leadership and a new campaign of civil disobedience began, though on a smaller scale than before. By November 1941, Nehru and 12,000 Congressmen were behind bars again and Congress ministries refused to operate in the states where they had been established.

Other groups began agitating for their various policies, and there was growing opposition to Congress from the Muslim League. The League was insisting on the establishment of a separate, independent Muslim state called Pakistan. The British refused to make any concessions until the various conflicting groups in India should speak with one voice. They continued, though, to promise full dominion status after the war

Gandhi listening to Muslim grievances.

to a United India. In December 1941, shortly before Japan entered the war, the government released all the Congress prisoners.

After the fall of Singapore the Japanese, in 1942, advanced through Burma. Even the threat of a Japanese invasion of India did not reconcile the Congress and the Muslim League. By this time, Indians were divided into two camps, those who wanted to help to defend India from the Japanese and those who looked upon them as possible liberators.

The situation in Asia was serious for Britain, and the British government thought that a gesture of conciliation would help to bring all Indians loyally behind the war effort. To this end a British mission under Stafford Cripps was sent to India to repeat the promise of dominion status after the war, but with the additional right of India to withdraw from the Commonwealth. The Congress leaders in India were not prepared to accept a 'post-dated cheque' from a bank which looked like going under. Many of them argued that they would do better in future negotiations with the Japanese if it was seen that they had been unhelpful to the British. So the Cripps mission failed.

In August 1942, Congress declared a 'Quit India' campaign. The Mahatma, foreseeing violence and wanting to act urgently to prevent it, asked for an interview with the Viceroy. This was refused. Instead, the Congress leaders were all arrested and imprisoned.

Violence broke out all over India. There was sabotage, murder and looting. Within a month, 250 railway stations had been destroyed and 500 post offices attacked. Police stations and government offices were set on fire. It was a rebellion, but fortunately not a general one, for the majority of Indian civilians in field and factory were receiving good pay and the men in the army supported the government.

Some British opinion laid the blame for the violence which had occurred upon the Mahatma. From prison he wrote to the Viceroy, Lord Linlithgow, strongly denying any responsibility. The Viceroy did not agree with him. At the end of 1942 the Mahatma wrote again asking the Viceroy why he had not tried negotiation before imprisoning and wronging innocent men. It was this hasty action which had provoked the violence and the Mahatma said that he would fast again. The Viceroy said that this was 'political blackmail' but nevertheless offered to release the Mahatma and all the Congress leaders. The offer was refused and the Mahatma fasted for almost three weeks.

Early in 1944 his wife Kasturbai died and a few weeks later the Mahatma became very ill with malaria. Agitation for his release was widespread, and in May he and all his Congress colleagues were let out of jail.

In June 1944, the Mahatma asked the new Viceroy, Lord Wavell, for a conference but this was refused. The Mahatma now tried to produce a combined front with Muhammad Ali Jinnah, the leader of the Muslim League, hoping that if Congress and the League could come together the British would be forced to yield power. Jinnah, however, had his mind fixed on the creation of Pakistan and refused to co-operate.

In May 1945, the war against Germany ended and in July a Labour government under Clement Attlee was elected in Britain. This government announced its intention to proceed without delay to the granting of self-government to India. Wavell was summoned to London for talks and on his return he restored provincial rule to the Congress ministries which had lapsed. He called together an assembly to draft a constitution, and set up a joint Hindu–Muslim executive council to decide on measures to prevent communal strife. Jinnah would accept nothing less than the partition of India into separate Hindu and Muslim states; the Mahatma regarded this as 'blasphemy'. From now on Jinnah, not the British, became his greatest difficulty.

below: *A street in north Calcutta on 28 August 1946 after British troops had been brought in to control the area.*

In March 1946, a British Cabinet Mission arrived to prepare the programme for the political changes necessary to ensure a smooth handing over of power to Indian politicians. The Mission asked for assistance from Congress and the Muslim League, but because these parties could not agree the Mission drafted its own plan in May. The Mahatma read the document and said: 'this is the best document the British government can produce in the circumstances and it shows a firm resolve to end British rule as soon as possible'.

The Mission had decided against the partition of India. Among the chief provisions were: a united India with a federal government: a federal Parliament with safeguards for religious minorities; and provincial governments with wide powers.

There was to be a constituent assembly called to draft the Constitution of India, and it would have three sections, one each for the Hindu and Muslim majority areas and the third for delegates from the mixed regions of Bengal and Assam. These were to be, in effect, the three sub-federations of India. Jinnah, not believing that the plan would be put into effect, accepted it to throw Congress into confusion. Although the Mahatma had reservations about the plan he urged Congress to accept it. This they refused to do because they feared that it would still lead to the division of India. Jinnah withdrew his acceptance, putting the blame for the failure of the plan on Congress. He now pressed on even more strongly with his claim for a separate Pakistan.

right: *Jinnah (extreme right, speaking into the microphone) with Nehru (second from left) at a reception at India House, London, 6 December 1946.*

below: *A victim of the riots in Calcutta 24 August 1946.*

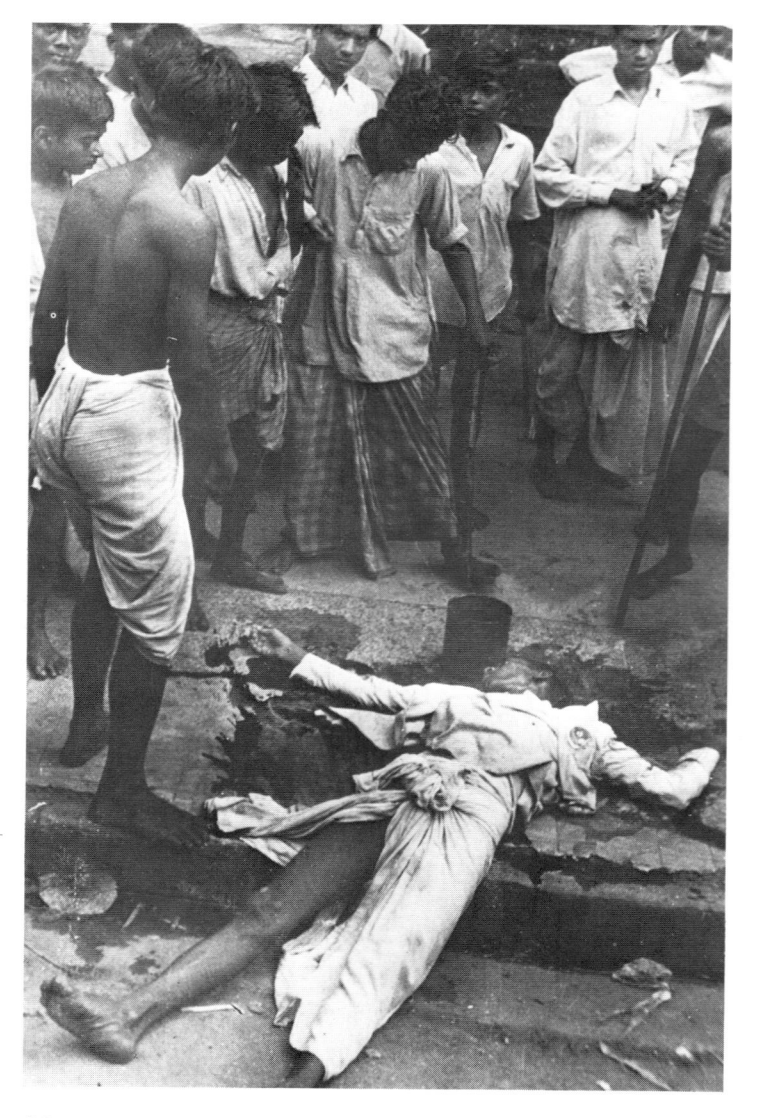

Wavell continued to try. He asked Congress and the Muslim League to assist in forming a federal government. Jinnah refused to take part and Wavell called on Nehru to form a government. Nehru offered Jinnah a senior appointment and the Mahatma even suggested that Jinnah should be Prime Minister, but he rejected all efforts to win him over. His answer was to declare 'Direct Action Day' on 16 August. This meant riots, and in the disturbances that followed 5,000 people were killed and 25,000 injured in Calcutta alone. Nehru became Prime Minister of India in September 1946. Jinnah proclaimed a day of mourning and the Hindu–Muslim rioting spread.

11 Hatred and partition

Reports reached the Mahatma of religious riots in the Noakhali region of East Bengal, where Muslims were forcibly converting Hindu men and ill-treating Hindu women. He decided to go there. On his way thousands of people crowded the stations to receive his blessing and he toured Calcutta, torn apart by rioting, to try to restore men to sanity.

Meanwhile in Bihar, Hindus, inflamed by exaggerated accounts from Noakhali, turned on the Muslims and killed more than 10,000. Going there, the Mahatma addressed crowds of Hindus. He urged that a mark of any people's civilisation was the way they treated minorities in their midst; and by this test the Biharis had shown themselves savages. He filled them with shame at their murderous conduct and threatened to fast if the riots continued. Nehru came also and was full of anger at what he saw. He threatened to bomb the rioters if they did not disperse.

Then the Mahatma went to Noakhali and for several months walked from village to village, enduring the greatest hardships and fatigue, sharing the lives of the people and urging them to live in peace. He was now in his seventy-seventh year. Of this time he wrote: 'My present mission is the most difficult of my life.'

In February 1947 the British government announced that Britain would give up her control over India by a date not later than June 1948. If this was an attempt to make the Congress and the Muslim League resolve their differences by a sense of urgency it failed. A new Viceroy was also sent, to try to make negotiations easier; he was Lord Mountbatten, a relative of the royal family and formerly commander-in-chief against the Japanese. But the affairs of India moved with ever-increasing speed. Jinnah warned Mountbatten that a civil war would engulf India if the Muslims were denied a separate state of Pakistan. The Viceroy conferred frequently and patiently with Jinnah, the Mahatma and Nehru. Jinnah utterly refused to accept the possibility of a United India which both Mountbatten and Congress desired. Congress was willing to accept partition, however, if only by that means could civil war be averted.

The Partition of India was not a simple matter. In the Punjab and Bengal, where there were large Muslim communities, there were also great numbers of Hindus and so these states had to be divided. The Mahatma could not agree to the dismemberment of India, but he was no longer able to influence developments. In the disturbances which accompanied the Partition, tens of millions of Hindus and Muslims became refugees and at least a million were murdered. India in the end did not respond to his call for peace and brotherhood and sadly he said, 'My thirty-two years of work have come to an inglorious end.'

On 15 August 1947, India celebrated her independence

Gandhi crossing a bridge during his peace-making visit to Noakhali.

Lord and Lady Mountbatten with Gandhi at the Viceroy's house, Delhi, 31 March 1947.

India, about 1950

Boundaries after Indian independence 15 Aug. 1947
Majority of Hindus
Majority of Muslims
Majority of other religions
Hindu minority 20-30%
Muslim minority 10-25%
Muslim minority 5-10%

within the British Commonwealth; Mountbatten had been invited to stay on as Governor-General, that is the British king's official representative in the new Dominion of India. The Mahatma felt unable to take part in the celebrations but stayed instead in Calcutta trying to stop Indians, both Hindus and Muslims, from killing one another. The Partition of Bengal had caused more problems than it solved, and Hindus and Muslims were in constant fear of attack from each other.

On 1 September, the Mahatma started to fast again. Three days later it was announced that no incidents had occurred throughout the previous twenty-four hours and that prominent Hindus and Muslims were calming their followers. Hundreds of policemen and their British officers joined the Mahatma in his fast, while remaining on duty. The community leaders, Muslim, Sikh and Hindu came to the Mahatma, and promised that there would be no more trouble. He asked them to write this promise and to sign it. They did so. When, later, the Punjab was convulsed by killing, Bengal kept its promise to the Mahatma and remained calm.

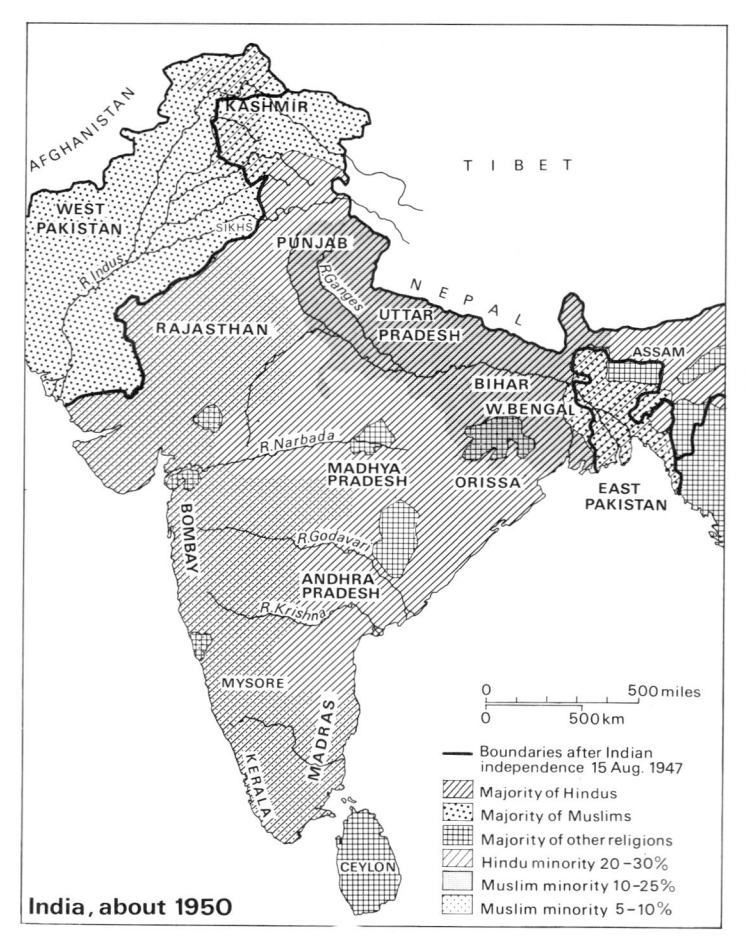

On 11 September, the Mahatma left for the Punjab. On his way he heard that Hindu refugees crowding into Delhi

right: *The Mahatma's body lying in state, 30 January 1948.*

below right: *The Gandhi memorial in Delhi, on the site of his funeral pyre.*

from the Punjab were killing Muslims there. He went to help and by arguing, teaching and scolding the people he was able to bring peace to some areas of the city. Violence against Muslims continued, however, and he began yet another fast on 13 January 1948. He said: 'death for me would be a deliverance rather than that I should be a helpless witness to the destruction of India'.

After three days he was in great pain. On 18 January a large delegation representing all the religions of India, and including the principal politicians, guaranteed that the lives and property of Muslims would be protected. Messages came from officials in every part of India.

Finally, the Mahatma agreed to take something to drink. Prayers from the Hindu and Muslim books were read and Christian hymns were sung. It was astonishing how the Mahatma, a frail old man, recovered from these dangerous fasts. He seemed to have complete mastery over his body which he had taken so often to the point of death. He was fired by an indomitable spirit and suffused by his love of God and of mankind.

Two days after his fast was over the Mahatma was addressing a prayer meeting when a bomb which had been thrown at him exploded harmlessly some distance away. Hindu extremists who were angry at the Mahatma's defence of Muslims were plotting to kill him. They wanted to reconquer Pakistan for India. He was the obstacle which stood in the way of war and hatred.

On 30 January in the early evening he walked, supported by two of his young disciples, into the garden to address the huge crowd which gathered there every evening to hear him. People touched his feet as he passed by. An assassin had moved into the front of the crowd and as the Mahatma approached he stood in front of him and bowed deeply. He then fired straight into the Mahatma's chest. The Mahatma's arms which were raised in blessing, fell to his sides and murmuring *'Hey Rama!'* ('O God'), he fell dead.

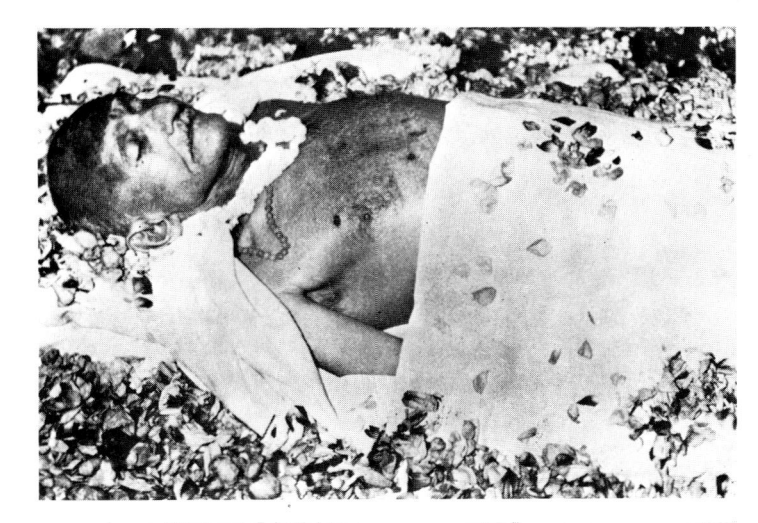

On the same evening Jawaharlal Nehru made the broadcast quoted on page 4 and continued:

'The light has gone out, I said, and yet I was wrong. For the light that shone in this Country was no ordinary light. The light which has illuminated this Country these many years will do so for many more years and a thousand years later that light will still be seen and the world will see it and it will give solace to countless hearts.'

12 The legacy of the Mahatma

In the years that have passed since Gandhi's death, India has undergone considerable turmoil and change. There have been three wars with Pakistan which has itself lost its eastern region so that there are now three independent nations in the Indian sub-continent. There has been a border war with China and a waxing and waning of the influence of Soviet Russia. Internationally, India is among the leaders of the non-aligned countries and she remains a member of the Commonwealth.

India has had two 'revolutions' also. There has been the black revolution of massive industrialisation and the green revolution of self-sufficiency in food. India has become an important exporter of industrial technology to less developed countries. Her railway system is itself the biggest single employer of labour in a nation which by 1979 numbered 680,000,000 people. She has a nuclear power industry which is capable of producing the hydrogen bomb. India has by far the largest and most profitable cinema industry in the world.

In spite of the continuing pressures of political corruption, poverty, over-population and vast unemployment she remains, strongly, a democracy. There have been mass movements to the towns and cities of villagers seeking a share of urban prosperity but still 80% of her people live in the countryside.

But much has not changed at all. In spite of the pious platitudes of politicians and their lip service to Gandhian ideals, there are 80,000,000 Untouchables still. Certainly they have rights under the constitution, but society has not yet changed sufficiently to allow them the use of all the wells or the solace of praying in the temples.

Obvious relics of the British period remain. English is still the public language of the educated Indians who, at home, might speak one of two hundred actual or fourteen official languages. The civil service is efficient, disinterested and, on the whole, incorruptible. The army is loyal to whatever government the people decide to elect and the generals do not seek political power.

So how much of what the Mahatma taught – he preferred to be called Bapu – has been carried on into modern times? He seems to be more honoured in his memory than in any specific policies of government. The realities of existing and competing in the modern world demand a degree of industrialisation which he would have resisted. Though there are some signs of industry spreading to the village communities, few people weave their own clothes. Gandhi's books have been burnt by modern revolutionaries who seek a more violent solution to India's problems.

What does remain is the example of his life and of his teaching, and his 'presence' as a statue in the centre of almost every town. He is still revered in the villages where his picture is often set beside that of Krishna. His name is on the lips of politicians at election times. He has become a kind of demi-god or hero, like Rama, the ruler of an ideal world of truth and justice and compassion.

No man did more than he to bring about the end of European empires. He ensured that India, however she would be governed, well or ill, would be governed by Indians themselves.

As a philosopher his autobiography, *The Story of my Experiments with Truth*, advocated a search for truth through action. As a man of action he has influenced the changing shape of the world. Before Lenin and Mao Tse Tung, his invention of Satyagraha became the disciplined basis of a struggle to improve the condition of men. It is still practised in India and in other parts of the world where oppressed minorities seek to achieve change without violence.

Although some of his ideas seemed absurd at the time, he succeeded in changing the attitude of countless millions of the downcast to one of self-respect and freedom. Religion and politics were to be combined in a common search for truth. The holy man was to come down from his remote mountain to undertake, with his own hands, the practical correction of the injustices of the world.